D1709577

THUNDERBIRD

FORD'S HIGH FLIER

BY JAY SCHLEIFER

EDISON MEDIA CENTER

Crestwood House
New York
Maxwell Macmillan Canada
Toronto
Maxwell Macmillan International
New York   Oxford   Singapore   Sydney

Crestwood House
Macmillan Publishing Company
866 Third Avenue
New York, NY 10022

Maxwell Macmillan Canada, Inc.
1200 Eglinton Avenue East
Suite 200
Don Mills, Ontario M3C 3N 1

Macmillan Publishing Company is part of the Maxwell Communication
Group of Companies.

First Edition
Produced by Twelfth House Productions
Designed by R Studio T

Printed in the United States of America

10   9   8   7   6   5   4   3   2   1

Library of Congress Cataloging-in-Publication Data

Schleifer, Jay.
Thunderbird / by Jay Schleifer.—1st ed.
    p.   cm.—(Cool classics)
Summary: Discusses the history and dynamics of the popular
American sports car.
ISBN 0-89686-816-8
1. Thunderbird automobile—History—Juvenile literature.
[1. Thunderbird automobile—History.]   I. Title   II. Series
TL215.T46S35   1994
        629.222'2—dc20   93-17241

CONTENTS

With its jet-pod styling, this 1962 Thunderbird is ready for takeoff!

① FLIGHT TIME

It's 6:00 A.M. and the sun is peeking over the eastern hills as you step out the door. Sure, it's chilly now, you think as you zip your leather jacket. But the sun will warm things up just fine. It's going to be a perfect day for flying.

Standing by is your Bird. Its sky blue finish gleams. Its long, wind-shaped lines look as if they're already moving. But it will take your skilled touch at the controls to make this baby really spread its wings.

Now you're inside and buckling up. A touch of the starter brings the engine to life. You can feel its muscle right through the soundproofing, as it turns over with soft-spoken power.

Time for a preflight check. The aircraft-type instruments before you report everything.

Fuel...full. Temp...coming up nicely. Oil pressure and volts...clean and green. You're cleared for takeoff.

You click the selector into place and take off. Flight time!

The description above could fit a private jet. But your flight today is ground-bound. You're about to take off in a classic, rocket-lined 1961 Ford Thunderbird.

For some 40 years, the T-Bird has been the stuff of car lovers' dreams. Some models have been tight-handling two-seat **road-sters.** Others have been luxury liners. Some of the latest have been powerful road brawlers. And still others, like this pod-shaped '62 model, have been amazingly aircraftlike in their streamlined looks and cloud-soft ride.

You're now invited to relive the story of all these memorable Thunderbirds. How do you do it? Easy!

Just spread your magic wings and fly...

The original two-seat T-Bird looked like no other sports car.

V-8, with a respectable 198 horsepower. But instead of just spinning the wheels, the engine would also be used to power luxury features. This car would be loaded with power steering, power brakes, even power seats and windows if the buyer ordered them.

Ford refused to call the new machine a sports car. The company called it a **personal car.** "The kind of car," Frank Hershey said later, "that a bank president or head of a company could drive without people saying, 'Look who still thinks he's a kid!'"

As Hershey and Boyer shaped the car's design, chief engineer Bill Burnett shaped its moving parts. Burnett knew that Ford had little experience with two-seaters. So as an experiment, he took a blowtorch to a regular Ford sedan. Burnett cut the car down from four seats to two. The result looked like something from a cartoon. But it taught Burnett how two-seaters move on the road.

It also gave the other engineers a joke. They called Ford's first two-seater the Burnetti.

When the design was finally finished, it was time to name the car. Ford asked its advertising company to come up with some choices. But none of the suggestions sounded right. So Ford held a contest among its workers. The prize was a $250 suit of clothes.

Ford would have lost its shirt on some of the entries. They included Fordette, Fordster, Detroiter, and Wheelaway! And those were among the best suggestions. Then there were the worst. One animal lover decided the perfect name would be Beaver. Another employee suggested the Hep Cat.

But in this stack of wacky ideas was one name that was perfect. It came from a designer named Alan "Gib" Giberson. He'd gotten it from a legend of the Native Americans of the Southwest. The legend described a magical bird of great power and beauty. The name was Thunderbird.

4 WINDOW WARS

January 1953 rolled around, and the new Corvette had finally been shown. Now Ford designers could compare their car with GM's.

What they saw must have brought tears of joy to their eyes. The Ford was better in lots of ways.

- Where the new Thunderbird had a V-8 engine, the Corvette offered only six-cylinder power.

- Where Ford gave customers a choice between automatic or stick shift, the Corvette was built one way—with an automatic transmission.

- Ford was offering the car with a removable hardtop. When the top was on, the car was weathertight. But on sunny days, the top could be left in the garage. The car also included the usual folding soft top for sudden rainstorms. The Corvette only offered the standard roof.

- The Ford body was steel, which was more familiar at the time to car buyers and body shops than the **fiberglass** body on Chevy's car.

- Where the Thunderbird offered all sorts of mechanical assists for steering, brakes, and seats, the Vette required muscle power. That meant that most of the car's operations were manual.

Perhaps most amazing to Ford were the Corvette's side windows. The car had none! Instead, Chevy used a pair of see-through plastic sheets called **side curtains.** You stuck them into holes on the top of the door. When you weren't using them, you had to store the curtains in the trunk.

Unlike the Corvette, the 1955 Thunderbird was available with a removable hardtop.

British sportsters had used side curtains for years. But Ford knew that luxury-loving American buyers would never stand for storing their windows in the car's trunk.

Not only did the new Ford have real windows, but a buyer could get the car with *power* windows. Each pane rolled up and down at the touch of a button!

By this time, Hershey and his designers loved their little car. They were especially pleased at how clean they'd made its lines, with just a touch of **chrome.** (This was a time when designers usually caked on chrome wherever they could.)

Then Hershey went on vacation. Big mistake!

While he was away, one of Ford's top bosses stopped by to see what all the "thunder" was about. He liked the car, but he had a suggestion. To make it look more like other Fords of the time, the designers needed to put a big, gloppy slab of chrome trim on the side.

"I blew my stack when I saw it!" Hershey remembered later. Then he marched straight to Henry Ford II, the head of the company.

His message to "HFII" was clear. The glob had to go. And the glob went. The manager who had asked for it, however, kept the chrome pieces. Later, he rode around with them on his own custom Thunderbird!

 **PORTHOLES AND SPARES**

In the new Thunderbird, Ford was sure it had a hit. And Ford was right. The T-Bird, as everyone now called it, was first shown at the 1954 Detroit Auto Show. Soon after, the phones at the dealers began to ring off the hook. How soon can I get one? would-be buyers wanted to know. How much will it cost?

When the car did go on sale, as a 1955 model, the price was $2,695—about the same as a Corvette. But while Corvettes just sat in showrooms, T-Birds flew right out the door.

Ford sold 16,155 cars that first year, far more than the 10,000 they had hoped for. Even more amazing, they sold at least *16 T-Birds for every Corvette sold.* Chevy had never been beaten that badly. And the Vette designers were determined not to let it happen again in 1956.

The '56 Vette was completely redone. It had a powerful V-8 engine. It had a new stick shift gearbox. It even had a removable hardtop and real roll-down windows. These improvements did help Chevy. That year Ford beat the Vette by only 5 to 1.

America had fallen in love with the T-Bird. People liked its neat but sporty look, its luxury touches, and its performance. "Ford is the first to say it's not so," wrote road test expert Walt Woron, "but they have a *sports car.* The more I drove it, the more I liked it."

In fact, there were only a couple of things buyers didn't like. It was hard to see out the rear when the hardtop was in place. And the spare tire took up most of the trunk. There was no place to put the golf clubs.

So in 1956, Ford fixed both problems. Engineers cut a set of boatlike **porthole** windows in the top. And the spare tire was hung out behind the trunk on what's called a **continental mount.** That solution brought on its own problem, though. All that weight so far back made the car tail-heavy. So in 1957 the new model got a stretched trunk—big enough for the spare *and* the golf clubs.

The '57 also got a major kick under the hood. The V-8 engine was made bigger and more powerful. Horsepower rose from under 200 to 245. And a special model had even more horses. It featured a **supercharger**—a pump that rammed an extra dose of gas-air mix down the V-8's throat. That kicked horsepower up to a nice, round 300! It also knocked the wind out of the driver as the

The 1957 model was the last of the two-seaters.

car rocketed from 0 to 60 miles per hour in just 5.5 seconds. That kind of speed was usually found only in expensive European sports cars like the Porsche or the Ferrari.

But changes to the Bird were just beginning. And they included one that would totally change the car's size and shape. The age of the original two-seat Thunderbird was ending. The age of the "Squarebird" was about to begin.

WANT MORE? TRY FOUR!

As the first-year sales figures rolled in, the numbers thrilled Frank Hershey and his designers. But in Ford's top offices, someone else was reading the numbers, too.

The man's name was Robert S. McNamara. He was the new top manager at Ford. In McNamara's opinion the two-seat Bird was a dead duck. In fact, he planned to kill the car off as soon as possible!

McNamara liked the car, as did almost everyone at Ford. But he also felt that the number sold was too small to be worth the time and money the company was spending on the car. So what if Ford sold 16,000 Thunderbirds in one year? The company's giant factories made 16,000 sedans every few hours. McNamara wanted his employees working on cars that sold 100,000 a year, not 16,000!

An old-time car company boss might have kept the Bird alive just for the love of it. But Bob McNamara was a numbers guy, not a car guy. If the T-Bird couldn't bring its sales numbers up, then he didn't want the company wasting time on it.

But maybe there was a way to increase sales. For the next new design—the '58 model—McNamara decided to make the T-Bird into a four-seater.

That way, families could buy the car *and* have a place to put the kids. Sure, the designers told McNamara that sporty cars were supposed to be two-seaters. But the numbers gave him a different message.

McNamara had another reason for changing to four seats. The company was just begining a new way of making cars called **unit body.** With this method there would no longer be a need for a big, heavy frame to hold up the car's body. The body itself would be strong enough to support all the car's parts. The new design would make the car both lighter and less costly to build.

Ford had set up a new factory to build its big Lincoln luxury sedans with unit bodies. McNamara figured that a four-seat T-Bird could share parts with the Lincoln and be built in the same factory. Manufacturing the cars together would help pay for the machinery faster. It would also make the Thunderbird cheaper to build. All the numbers said to make the change—and do it as soon as possible.

But McNamara's decision was not popular at Ford. When fans of the two-seater T-Bird heard about the plan, their tempers went into overdrive. They didn't want to turn their beloved roadster into a kind of sedan. One worker was so upset he called another company to ask about getting the two-seaters made there—outside of Ford! Within half an hour the man was summoned to McNamara's office.

You can imagine Bob McNamara sitting behind his huge desk, his eyeglasses glinting in the office light. The wayward employee understood that he was attending the two-seater's funeral. "It's dead," said the Ford boss sternly. "I don't ever want to hear of it again." **19**

(7) CLEARED FOR TAKEOFF

When the designers began to work on the new Thunderbird, they were pleasantly surprised. They actually had fun with the new model.

Without a frame underneath, the seats could be dropped deep inside the shell. There would still be a high ridge right down the middle, between the front seats, covering the drive shaft. But the ridge neatly divided the front seats into two airplanelike cockpit areas.

Then somebody had a brainstorm. Put controls on top of the ridge! That made it look like the control panel of a jet. Today we call this panel a **console,** and it's on lots of cars. But the four-seat T-bird was the first to have it.

Once they got hooked on the aircraft idea, the designers really began to soar. They gave the hood the flatness of an airport runway. They copied the control levers right out of a 707 airliner. And, of course, they put tail fins on the rear. With a little imagination, drivers could really feel as if they were cleared for takeoff.

And because there were four seats, designers decided to group other parts in fours as well. The T-Bird was the first car to have four headlights. It had four huge round taillights, too. For the T-Bird, four was the magic number.

Buyers of convertibles got even more. On most **ragtops** of the time, the top folded down and formed a big lump of cloth and metal rods behind the backseat. The styling didn't do much for the car's lines.

But on the new Bird, the top totally vanished into the trunk. It was swallowed by a huge lid that opened behind the backseat like an alligator's mouth. When the mouth closed, the car's lines were left pure and clean.

Of course, convertible buyers also got less trunk room. The top, plus all the motors to make this magic happen, filled most of the space. But for fans of the open road, it didn't matter. If they wanted the wind in their hair, they'd have to travel light!

Owners of hardtops (nonremovable this time) had a pretty unusual roof, too. Most cars of the 1950s had tops that sloped down to the trunk. But the T-Bird's designers made their top square and boxy, like a stately home or a government building. The design had a classy look. It also gave backseat passengers easier entry and more headroom.

The "Squarebird," with four seats, boosted Thunderbird sales. Many people hated it, but it kept the car alive!

Ford knew that its square look was different. "It was quite a shock, frankly, to see it," said Gale Halderman, a top designer. "You had to take a second look. But it became so popular they put it on the [full-size] Ford sedans a few years later."

The squarish roof also helped lead to the car's nickname—the "Squarebird."

When the Squarebird hit the market, lovers of the two-seater growled. But McNamara's numbers turned out to be on the money. Sales doubled the first year out. After that, there was no stopping the Bird!

By 1960, almost 91,000 four-seaters were being built a year. That was six times what the car had sold as a two-seater. Ford had made a tremendous breakthrough in the car business. It had designed the first sporty four-seater.

In the next few years other companies followed with cars like the Pontiac Grand Prix and the Buick Riviera. They copied the T-Bird's twin cockpit seating, its control panel between the seats, and its squarish roof.

Ford followed, too, with a lower-priced four-seat sportster called the Mustang. Some called it the Poor Man's Thunderbird.

By 1961, though, Ford decided that it was time for a new Thunderbird design. Right now the company was selling the most popular sporty four-seat car. But what could the designers pull from their bag of tricks to keep that lead?

 **ROAD ROCKET**

Ten…nine…eight…seven…six… In 1961, countdowns were in. The space race had begun. U.S. and Soviet scientists were competing to see who could build the best rockets. Each country

The "Squarebird" got its name from the shape of its roof.

wanted to put the first human in orbit (the Soviets won) and the first human on the moon (the United States won).

Designer Bill Boyer was now head of the Thunderbird team. As he watched the rocket launches on TV, he toyed with the design for the new Bird. And as he thought about it, he got a bright idea. If the Squarebird was like an airliner, the next Bird would look as if it could fly right into space. He would design a rocket for the road— a pointy-nosed missile for four. First, though, Boyer's car had to win its own space race—at the Ford factory.

Ford had decided to hold a contest to create the design for the

"Third Bird." And there was another designer trying for that honor. His name was Elwood Engel.

Engel worked on Lincolns and Mercurys. He saw the Thunderbird differently from the way Boyer did. To Engel, a T-Bird was a cool, classy piece of work. He didn't want to see it junked up with the chrome and fins of the time. He didn't want the design to shoot off into rocket mode. Instead, Engel wanted the Bird to remain a classic car with simple, beautiful lines.

Working in a basement room so narrow it was called the Submarine Service, Engel created the car of his dreams. Its sides were clean and flat. There wasn't a bump or curve that didn't

belong. And, Engel said, "I made sure it didn't have any of those big, heavy-looking bumpers and fins"—the kind Boyer was molding just a few flights of stairs away.

When both designs were ready, they were wheeled into a large room. It was up to Ford's top bosses to decide which would win the right to the road.

Henry Ford II, McNamara, and others paced and stared. They looked at the cars from front, back, and sides. They squinted and peered. This was no easy decision. Both cars were beautiful, each in its own way.

Finally they put their heads together and came up with a

surprising verdict. The company would build both cars. The Boyer rocket would win the Thunderbird badge. The Engel design would be made longer, get an extra set of doors, and become a Lincoln. In fact, it turned out to be the most successful Lincoln in years.

The T-Bird rocket moved onward toward production. Engineers gave it a massive, 300-horsepower, 390-cubic-inch V-8 engine. The **suspension** was improved over past four-seaters. And an automatic gearbox, power steering, and brakes were all made **standard.** Most buyers were choosing them, anyway.

When the car went on sale, magazine reviewers were impressed. "In front of your house, it will turn your neighbors green with envy," wrote *Car Life*.

The Thunderbird got its thunder from massive V-8s like this 390-inch monster. It's nearly *twice* as big as most of today's engines.

But Boyer—and Ford—knew that the new car still had to compete in the market. Other carmakers had finally caught on to the idea of the sporty four-seater. Over the next few years, General Motors brought out the Pontiac Grand Prix, Chevy Monte Carlo, Olds Toronado, and Buick Riviera. All were sporty four-seat cars. Some were priced lower than the T-Bird, some higher. The Ford was surrounded in the market. Sales dropped.

Ford expected the loss and kept trying out new ideas to keep its lead. The company also tried one old idea: Turn the four-seater back into a two-seater!

No, it didn't bring back the car McNamara had promised would remain dead. Instead, designers created a huge plastic panel that simply bolted into place over the backseat. Maybe they hoped that by hiding the backseat, the car would again be the compact, sweet-handling machine that had made the T-Bird name famous. This creation was called the Sports Roadster.

Needless to say, it didn't work. Only about 1,400 Roadsters were built out of a total 1962 production of about 78,000 T-Birds. A couple of years later the number had fallen to just 50 "two-seat four-seaters" sold in a year. The idea was dropped.

In 1964 the rocket was redesigned by adding a dose of Squarebird to its flowing lines. Under the skin everything was pretty much the same. But there were a couple of new features, too.

One was a three-light rear turn signal. When the driver hit the control, the lights flashed in order. They started from the middle of the car and moved in the direction of the turn. It was like a moving arrow pointing the way.

The look was fantastic. But it could also startle other motorists or take their attention from their own driving. After a few years, the T-Bird was back to a single flashing red light.

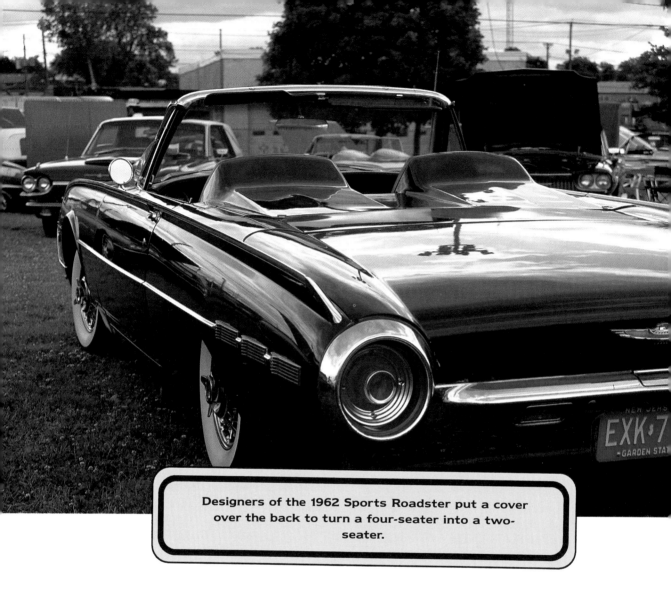

Designers of the 1962 Sports Roadster put a cover over the back to turn a four-seater into a two-seater.

Although the new square rocket made sales jump, profits fell by the next year. Ford knew that more basic changes to the T-Bird were needed. But what would they be?

The top man at Ford would have to decide. But McNamara had left the company to work for the government. Ford now had a new chief executive. He would become famous in the years to come, first at Ford and later at Chrysler.

His name was Lee Iacocca.

9 "THUNDERBULK"

To understand what happened to the T-Bird next, you need to know how Lee Iacocca got into the car business. Back in the 1940s, Lee was a student at Lehigh University in Pennsylvania. Like most students, he wasn't quite sure what to do with his future.

One day a Ford recruiter came to the college. He was looking for bright young people to join his company. The man arrived in a Lincoln Continental, Ford's best car at the time.

Lee was floored by the long, lavish lines of the big Lincoln. Growing up poor, he'd seldom seen a car like that. And Lee never forgot the impression it made. Perhaps it was at that moment that Lee became a big-car guy—a big-car guy who would one day have his company build a big Thunderbird!

In fact, the Bird had been putting on weight for years. The original two-seater tipped the scales at 3,570 pounds. That was about average for a U.S. car of the time but heavier than the European two-seaters. Then a steady diet of size, chrome, and fins had eventually added more than 500 pounds. The T-Bird had now broken the two-ton barrier. And, as is the case with a chubby athlete, the extra weight had slowed down both speed and handling.

However, the eating binge was just beginning. For his new model, Iacocca demanded another increase in size. Some GM four-seaters were even bigger than the T-Bird. And Iacocca wanted to keep up.

Designers weren't happy, and it showed. The creature they rolled out in 1967 was a jumble of eight separate ideas. The front end looked like a large metal mouth sticking out of a chunky body. The once classy roof was now just a big box—usually covered with fake leather. It sat on top of a larger box that was the car's body.

Under Lee Iacocca, the Thunderbird grew two extra doors and a beak! The four-door model lasted only a few years.

The rear end was a slab of red plastic. The whole car just seemed to sag on its wheels.

The sleek convertible was gone, a victim of safety rules and air-conditioning. And the model that replaced it was the most *un*-Thunderbird yet. The car, built to Iaccoca's orders, was a *four-door sedan!*

While designers pouted, Iacocca smiled. "The bigger it got, the better he liked it," says Gale Halderman, one of Ford's best designers. "It seemed that every pound was better."

Sure, some people liked their wheels high-tech and compact. But other buyers just wanted a famous name and a lot of car for the money. And Lee Iacocca was a master salesman who really knew car buyers. It was no surprise then that, as Halderman says, "every time we made it bigger, it seemed it sold a little better."

 **COOKIE CUTTER CARS**

In the early 1970s cars were shaped by more than just what buyers wanted. During this time the United States had a dispute with some of the oil-producing countries in the Middle East. As a result, the producers stopped selling America their oil. Gasoline was suddenly hard to get. Lines stretched for blocks at the few service stations that had fuel to sell. And prices doubled.

Suddenly, small, gas-saving cars were *in!* Sales of all big cars, including the huge "Thunderbulk," as some now called it, dropped sharply. It was clear that car companies had to start building smaller models.

Iacocca knew just how to make this situation work for Ford. In 1977 he stopped making the T-Bird as a special model on its own. Instead, he turned it into a fancy version of an ordinary midsize Ford two-door sedan.

This new, smaller Bird had a color stripe that went up and over the roof. Designers called the stripe the basket handle. And, of course, the car had the Thunderbird name pasted all over it. Other than that, there was little difference between the Bird and the sedan. But the change did make the car much cheaper to build.

Now Iacocca and his sales department were able to make the one change in the Thunderbird that they really wanted. The company cut the price of the T-Bird by more than a third.

Suddenly Joe or Mary Average Car Buyer could afford to buy a *Thunderbird!*

Of course, it wasn't a special model as it had been before. It was the T-Bird name on an ordinary car. But that didn't seem to matter. Joe bought it, and so did Mary. Suddenly Ford was selling more than 300,000 T-Birds a year. It was a huge success for a car that had never sold more than about 90,000 until then.

But while the money rolled in, something was lost. In any auto company, the family cars pay the bills. But the special cars, like the T-Bird or Corvette or Jeep, give the company its soul. Without such cars, a company's products would be as exciting as washing machines. And when was the last time you saw the name of a washing machine company on a T-shirt or baseball cap?

For Ford, the Thunderbird was no longer a special car. And as its jazzy image faded, its popularity did, too.

Actually, in the early 1980s, buyers began to turn away from U.S. cars in general. Like the T-Bird, many cars had become little more than different nameplates on the same boring machine. Writers called it the "cookie cutter" look. Fords looked like Mercurys. You

The gasoline shortage of the early 1970s ended the days of big cars like this 1969 Thunderbird.

could hardly tell a Buick from a Cadillac. Even a car's name became less important. For instance, you couldn't even find the name of the car inside a Chrysler vehicle. The company put the label *Dodge* or *Plymouth* only on the outside.

When designers got their freedom, auto lovers got this streamlined beauty.

And that wasn't the U.S. companies' only problem. Buyers were fed up with how poorly many American cars were built. In Ford's case, someone even dug up the old 1920s joke that the name *Ford* stands for *"Fix Or Repair Daily!"*

At the same time, cars from other nations, especially Japan, now offered more. They were more comfortable. They got more miles to the gallon. They weren't more expensive. And they were also ahead in technology.

As U.S. sales dropped, Japanese sales quickly rose. Soon one of every four cars sold was an import like Toyota or Honda. Some people wondered if giant companies like Chrysler and even Ford would go out of business!

For Thunderbird, a new model in 1980 only made things worse. It was another box that even its designers hated.

"The 1980 Thunderbird had to be the worst U.S. car ever in the '70s and '80s," said Chris Cedergren, an auto industry expert. "It was awful design-wise, quality-wise....If I was head of Ford, I'd have [fired] everybody on the project. I would have said, 'You've got to be kidding! Get out of the building!'"

Other experts had other opinions. Some liked the car. But the ones who mattered most, the customers, turned away in droves. Sales of the T-Bird took a nosedive.

If this Bird was ever going to fly again, things had to change. And change they did!

 **THE AERO-BIRD**

You stand by the rail at the Daytona Speedway and listen. Suddenly, there it is—the sound of thunder. Or the sound of Thunderbirds, *to be more exact.*

Now you see them. Several boldly painted stock car racers, with the blue Ford oval painted on them. They're running nose to tail, inches apart, looking like the world's fastest express train. And they're reaching speeds of nearly 200 miles per hour.

*As they pass in less than a second, you notice their shape—smooth and rounded. The grille is swept back. The glass in the windows is even with the metal of the doors. The roof smoothly slopes into the rear. And a fin called a **spoiler** at the edge of the trunk tricks the air into thinking the shape is even more slippery than it is.*

The old boxy design is nowhere to be seen. It's 1983. And this is the new look of the Thunderbird.

As the 1970s ended, Lee Iacocca was pushed out of Ford and went to Chrysler. Then Henry Ford II retired. Now a new, younger breed of manager took over the company. Many of the new bosses were trained in Europe, where clean design and high-tech engineering—not chrome—sold cars.

One of those managers was Jack Telnack, the new boss of the Ford Design Center. Telnack looked over the cars on the drawing board and shook his head. Most had the old boxy look. Then he sat down with the designers. "I asked them what *they* thought the cars should look like," said Telnack. "This wasn't the way things were done back then. You waited for your boss to tell you what he thought the car should look like, then you drew it. But in time, they realized I was serious."

Suddenly designers were given their freedom. And one of the first cars on which they used it was the new 1983 Thunderbird.

First they junked the work already done on the car under the old system. Nobody cried over the lost work. The design was just another box, a little rounder than the one before.

Then the designers began sketching like mad to come up with something better. But they had only a short time before Ford was going to test it on the public.

As luck would have it, another crew at the Design Center had

The Turbo T-Bird made Ford's little four-cylinder
engine a force to be reckoned with.

been working on a new kind of Lincoln. It wasn't due out until after
the Thunderbird. Their vehicle was called the **Aero** Luxury Car. It
had the soft, rounded design that later become known as the "Ford
look." At last Lincoln had a chance to pay the Bird back for the
Lincoln design that had started out as a T-Bird back in the 1960s. It
was the Thunderbird's turn to borrow a design. And it did.

The Aero Luxury Car was rolled into the Ford design room. Then
the Ford crew tore into it. They removed the Lincoln lines and
added those that said T-Bird. Finally, the Aero-Bird model was
loaded on a truck and sent on its way.

Then came fingernail-biting time. Would buyers accept this
different-looking car as a Thunderbird? Would they understand
that curved lines would work better when the car moved through
the air? Would they believe this was better than the chrome boxes

they'd been told to buy for years? Or would they turn their backs and buy Japanese?

The buyers' decision was loud and clear. When the curtain went up, the audience cheered!

"We knew then we had a 1983 Thunderbird," says Gale Halderman.

Now it was the engineers' turn to give the car a performance equal to its looks. Buyers got a choice of three engines. The first engine was a mild-mannered V-6. The second was the same 302-cubic-inch **small block V-8** used in the Mustang. But the third choice was wilder. It was a four-cylinder engine with a **turbocharger.** Turbos punch up performance by ramming a gas-air mixture into the engine instead of letting it float in on its own.

And perform the Turbo-Coupe did. "Hot diggity, oh, boy!" said a writer from *Car and Driver* magazine after trying out one of the first models.

"This is the best Thunderbird in years," said *Road & Track*.

Magazines were thrilled by the car's wind-shaped new looks. And so was the **National Association of Stock Car Auto Racing.**

NASCAR teams were always looking for sleek new body shells to snap onto their racing **chassis**. The Aero-Bird was exactly what they wanted. It wasn't long before Birds were flying down the speedways at more than 200 miles per hour—and winning!

With top wheelman Bill Elliot aboard, new Thunderbirds took the NASCAR championships in 1985 and 1987. Elliot also set an incredible record at Daytona of 199.557 mph for 10 full laps—so close to the incredible 200 mph barrier.

As the 1980s went on, the rounded look of the Aero-Bird became the model for a whole family of Ford cars. You can see it in everything from the Escort to the Crown Victoria. But it shows up strongest in the Taurus, America's first real aero–family sedan.

Is it a Ford...or a BMW? The 1989 T-Bird took on a high-tech, luxury look.

Taurus was a huge gamble for Ford. The company spent more than $3 billion to build it. If it had failed, the company would probably have folded. But it was a giant success, partly, say Ford executives, because of the T-Bird. The Aero-Bird helped get buyers used to the new rounded shapes.

In 1992, in fact, Taurus did something American car companies had been dreaming about for a long time. It beat the Honda Accord out of the title of the best-selling car in America. Honda had held that title for years.

And it all began with the 1983 Thunderbird.

 **FUTURE FLIGHT**

In 1989, there was yet another new Bird...the sleekest, most high-tech yet. The car looked a lot like an expensive German BMW. One model, the SC Coupe, was even supercharged.

The latest Bird also featured **independent rear suspension (IRS).** That's a system in which each rear wheel is attached to the chassis in a way that allows it to take bumps without causing the other wheel to bounce. Handling improves as the tires stay in better contact with the road.

This car will probably be produced until the mid-1990s to late 1990s. But what flight plan will Thunderbird follow after that?

Of course, Ford won't tell. But based on concept cars at auto shows, here are some guesses at what you'll see on Thunderbirds
in the coming years:

- *Streamlining:* The car that made the aero look famous will continue to be shaped by the wind. Expect even rounder shapes and fewer parts sticking out into the airstream.
- *Engine:* Look for the T-Bird to offer powerful engines. But these may include **two-stroke** designs as well as the present **four-stroke.** Two strokes make power each time the engine turns instead of every other turn. They're smaller and lighter. Right now two strokes are used mostly in motorcycles, dirt bikes, and other small engines. They're noisy and smoky. But as engineers solve these problems, cars will begin using two-stroke designs more and more.
- *Driveline:* On an idea car called the Contour, Ford showed an unusual **T-drive system.** It takes power from the center of the engine instead of from the end. This design allows for both a sideways-mounted engine (as on front-wheel-drive cars), which gives good use of space, and rear drive, which is best for handling on a sporty car. What better car for the T-drive than the T-Bird?
- *Electronics:* The Thunderbird is already heavily computer controlled. In the future, electronics will be even more prominent on the Thunderbird.
- *Materials:* Today's cars are made mostly of steel and glass. In the future, look for more recyclable plastics and something called a **composite.** This mix of materials is now used on jet fighters like the F-16 and F/A-18. A composite offers both light weight and super strength.

   Whatever the combination of these features, Ford seems set on keeping the T-Bird in front of the pack. Or as Ted Finney, a design manager for this Cool Classic, puts it, "At one time, long ago, Thunderbird really meant something. We lost that for a while. Now I think the magic is back!"

Some people think Ford's Contour show car hints at the Thunderbirds of the twenty-first century.

 GLOSSARY/INDEX

continental mount 15 A method of storing a spare tire outside the trunk of a car and over the rear bumper.

fiberglass 11 A plasticlike material used in the body of the Corvette. Fiberglass is easy to work with and does not rust.

four stroke 45 An engine design that makes power every other turn. The design is now in use in almost all car and truck engines.

independent rear suspension (IRS) 44 A system of mounting the rear wheels so that if one hits a bump, the other stays in contact with the road.

National Association of Stock Car Auto Racing (NASCAR) 41 The official rule-making organization of stock car racing.

personal car 10 Ford's name for a two-seater or four-seater not built for super performance but for fun driving and luxury.

porthole 15 Round window usually found in the sides of ships.

ragtop 20 Slang for convertible.

roadster 5, 7, 19, 27, 28 A two-door, two-seat open sports car.

sedan 6, 41 A comfortable car designed to carry more than two passengers. Sedans often have four doors.

side curtains 11, 14 See-through plastic panels that mount on a sports car door and serve as windows. When not used, they are stored in the car's trunk.

small block V-8 41 A medium-powered eight-cylinder engine, usually with about 200 horsepower.

spoiler 39 A body-mounted fin that funnels the airflow around a car either to streamline it or to use air to force the car to the road.

standard 26 Referring to items included in the car's basic price. If priced extra, the items are called options.

supercharger 15, 44   An engine-driven pump that rams gas-air mixture into the motor, for extra power.

suspension 26, 44   Parts for mounting the wheels to a car. The suspension includes springs, shocks, and steering gear.

T-drive system 45   A Ford invention that draws power from the center of a sideways-mounted engine instead of from its end. This allows for the roominess of a front-drive car and the tight handling of a rear-drive design.

turbocharger 40, 41   A pump, driven by exhaust gas, that rams gas-air mixture into the engine for extra power.

two stroke 45   An engine design that makes power on every turn. The design is now mostly used in motorcycles and other small engines but is being experimented on for cars.

unit body 19   A way of building a car in which the body also acts as the frame. This type of design cuts weight and uses less metal.